Also by Evelyn McFarlane & James Saywell

If . . . (Questions for the Game of Life)
If² . . . (500 New Questions for the Game of Life)
If³ . . . (Questions for the Game of Love)

If . . .

Questions for the Soul

If . . .

Questions for the Soul

Evelyn McFarlane & James Saywell
Illustrated by James Saywell

Villard/New York

The authors would like to
dedicate this book to Italy,
which has been so good
for their souls.

If . . .

Questions for the Soul

At the center of each of us lies our essential spirit. It is what defines us, makes us individuals, and gives us our ultimate strength. It gives us hope for a greater purpose to the life we lead, and the yearning for a sense of meaning. This core in us is something everyone is born with and will die with, and it is what many believe carries forth *beyond* death. It is our soul.

It is unreachable in a literal sense—there is no one who can access it directly—but we inherently desire to know more about it, in order to better understand ourselves. If you could look into your soul, would you wish to? The ability to know ourselves involves great effort and courage, and is essential to the living of our lives.

While a soul cannot be asked a question directly—or answer one at any rate—this fourth collection of "If . . ." questions is designed to help us explore—at our own pace, and to varying depths—that most hidden and essential part of ourselves. It gently looks at the heart of our beliefs, fears, and hopes, as well as those of the people we love. Like all the *If . . .* books, the collection is intended to be used randomly, and we hope the questions will be shared and will give rise to enriching and revealing conversations and deeper knowledge of ourselves and others. We have included some lighter questions as well, not to offend, but to ease the weight of the collection as a whole, and to include one of life's most important ingredients—smiles—with the contemplation that we intend the others to generate.

May you find parts of yourself you weren't familiar with, and greet them with warm forgiveness.

If God were to grant you one favor, what would you ask?

If you could make one thing come true for the good of all souls on the planet, what would it be?

—⊷ ☰✧☰ ⊶—

If you had to name a time when you could say that you were spiritually repressed, when would it be?

—⊷ ☰✧☰ ⊶—

If you were to identify where the majority of your fears in life come from, what would you say?

If you could have changed one thing in the life of someone now deceased, what would it be?

—⊷ ⊶—

If Heaven had to look like the inside of one of your friends' homes, whose would you pick?

—⊷ ⊶—

If you could make one person you know more religious, who would you pick?

—⊷ ⊶—

If you could make one person in the world less religious, who would you select?

If you could have witnessed one religious event, which one would you choose?

⋯ ⋰ ⋯

If you could have asked Jesus one question, what would it be?

⋯ ⋰ ⋯

If there was a time when the death of someone touched your sense of mortality the most, when would it be?

If there was a time when, despite your resistance, a change in your life turned out to be for the better, when would you say it was?

7

If you found out you *did* have a guardian angel, what would you name it?

If you had to pick the single most spiritual moment of your life so far, when would it be?

———— ✠ ————

If you discovered that you were to die tomorrow, what would you do for the rest of today?

———— ✠ ————

If you were to say there was a time in your life when your emotional attachment to someone was detrimental, when would it be?

If tomorrow you lost the person you love most in the world, how would your life change?

If you had to name the single most important ingredient for a spiritual life, what would you say it is?

If you had to choose one way that God's existence could be proven to the world at large, what would be the most convincing?

If you could have God's existence personally proved to you in one way, what would it be?

If you could, for the good of mankind, reverse one scientific discovery or development, what would it be?

＋＋ ≡◆≡ ＋＋

If one thing you presently own were to become a religious relic, what would you pick?

If you decided today to do some serious soul searching, what would be the first question you'd ask yourself?

＋＋ ≡◆≡ ＋＋

If you were to sell your soul for one thing, what would you do it for?

If you had to pick the most sacred spot you've ever seen, where would it be?

If you were asked to make the case for the nonexistence of God, how would you begin?

If you were asked to make the case for the existence of God, what would be Exhibit A?

If you were to die tomorrow, how would you want to go?

11

If you were to assign people you know to represent each of the virtues and vices, who would be what?

If you had to honestly rate your own ego on a comparative scale of 1 to 10, with the average human scoring 5, where would you place it?

If you had to remember a time in your life when your own self-esteem was at its lowest, when would you say it was?

If you could take one possession with you into the afterlife (assuming there is one), what would you take?

If you were to be accompanied by anyone into the next world, who would you take?

If you could help one person you know find their inner spirit, who would it be?

If someone you know personally had to become the next pope, who would you want it to be?

If you had to cast the role of true evil in a new film, what actor would you select for the part?

If a good friend asked you to assist them with their suicide, how would you respond?

⚊⚌✦⚌⚊

If you were to learn that there actually is a Heaven and a Hell, what is the first thing you'd change in your life?

⚊⚌✦⚌⚊

If you could inherit any religious structure in the world, which would you choose?

If you were to construct a small altar somewhere in your home, where would you put it?

If someone you know had to become the next Dalai Lama, who would you want it to be?

If you decided to devote the next two years of your life to building a new church anywhere in the world, where would you put it?

If you were to name the single most important moment in history for organized religion, when would you say it was?

If you could determine one aspect of your own death, except its moment, what would it be?

If you had to name the best aspect of any single religion, what would it be?

If you had to name the worst aspect of any single religion, what would it be?

If you were to exchange souls for one day with someone you know, who would you want it to be with?

If you were to exchange souls for one day with someone from history, who would you pick?

16

If you had to name the one thing you most regret about your life up to this point, what would it be?

—————— ≍✦≍ ——————

If you were to write your own epitaph today, what would it say?

If you could have met one religious figure from history, who would you choose?

—————— ≍✦≍ ——————

If you could have met one figure from the Bible, who would you pick?

If you were to name the most spiritual person you know, who would it be?

If you had to name the least spiritual person you know, who would you elect?

If you had to name the moment in your life when you most needed the understanding of someone else, when would you say it was?

If you had to name the book that most touched your soul, which would you choose?

If you were to name the most spiritual of all current world political leaders, who comes to mind?

If you had to explain the difference between "religious" and "spiritual" in the simplest terms, what words would you use?

If you had to describe the ideal role of religion in modern society, what would you say?

If you could be buried or have your ashes spread anywhere on Earth, where would it be?

If you could add one thing to your life that you believe would make you more spiritual, what would it be?

If you had to eliminate one existing religion, which would you choose?

If you could undo one thing you've done in your life that has haunted you with guilt, what would it be?

If you had to recall the most insincere expression of faith you have ever come across, what would you say it was?

If you were to identify the one thing that you have always been the most superstitious about, what would it be?

＊＊ ＝◇＝ ＋＋

If you were to name the person who most surprised you with their faith, who would it be?

If you were to name the person you know who has the most ideal understanding of faith, who would it be?

＊＊ ＝◇＝ ＋＋

If you were to name the person who has given you true emotional strength, who would it be?

If you had to name one person you know who would make the most successful/convincing TV evangelist, who would it be?

If you were to become a monk or nun, which order would you enter, and where would you want to be?

— ≍◆≍ —

If you were to better yourself in one way, how would you do it?

— ≍◆≍ —

If you were asked for proof of your moral fiber, in what way or with what example would you establish it?

If you were to identify the inner need that your worst habit fulfills, what would it be?

—————— ✠ ——————

If you could give the pope one piece of advice, what would you tell him?

—————— ✠ ——————

If your soul were to be represented by a color, which color would it be?

—————— ✠ ——————

If you were to add an eleventh commandment, what would it be?

23

If you could have avoided knowing about one thing during your life, what would it be, and why?

If you were to choose one television show to be banned for moral reasons, which would you pick?

If you had to name the one thing about yourself that would be the most difficult to change, what would it be?

If you had to name the one thing about yourself that would be easiest for you to change but that you never have gotten around to, what would it be?

24

If your parents were to confess to you the most shocking thing you can imagine, what would it be?

If one of your children were to tell you the one thing that would most upset you, what would it be?

If you were in need of emotional refuge, what would you do to find it?

If you were to describe the time or activity that makes you feel most spiritual, what would you say it was?

25

If you could have learned one life lesson earlier than you did, which one would you want it to be?

＋＋ ✠ ＋＋

If you could teach someone you know one life lesson, who would it be, and what would they learn?

＋＋ ✠ ＋＋

If you had to name the cause that you believe is the most worthy on the planet, what would it be?

If you were to construct a small religious altar in your home using only three things you now own, what would they be?

26

If you could have the power to make one person you know tell only the truth forevermore, who would you choose?

If you promised to never lie again in your lifetime, in what area would it be the hardest to uphold the promise?

If you could make certain that your parents knew one thing before they died, what would it be?

If you could give one thing to all the senior citizens of the Earth, what would it be?

If you could change one thing about a single religion, which one would it be, and how would you alter it?

If you could have your parents hear one thing as they die, what would it be?

＋＋ ✦ ＋＋

If you had to describe the single most profound experience of your life so far, what would you say?

＋＋ ✦ ＋＋

If you had to name the one experience that strengthened your character the most so far, what would it be?

If you were to play a particular piece of music to make you feel contemplative, what would you put on?

※

If you were to plan the menu of your last supper, what would it be?

※

If you were to say that you have one doubt about your heart and soul, what would it be?

※

If you could wear one outfit from your present wardrobe to enter Paradise in, what would you pick?

29

If you could have someone famous read your eulogy, who would you choose?

If someone famous were to unexpectedly show up at your funeral, who would you want it to be?

If you could face one of your fears head-on and conquer it, which would you pick?

If you could change your identity completely, what would the new you be like?

If you could have anything happen to your body after you die, what would you want to occur?

If you could meet one person before dying whom you have never met, who would it be?

If you had to name the hardest transition you have had to make in life, what would you say?

If you were to found a spiritual retreat, where would it be located?

If you were to name the person with the best sixth sense, who would it be?

If you had to die in one of the places you have lived in your life, but not your present home, which spot would you choose?

If you could give one person you know a prize for goodness, who would receive it?

If you had to describe the one experience that weakened you the most, what would it be?

32

If you were to receive a prize for one aspect of your character, what would you want it to be for?

If you were to name a single thing that can destroy a soul, what would it be?

If you were to describe the most spiritual country you've ever been in, which would you choose?

If you were to describe the most spiritual place you can *imagine*, what would it be like?

If you had to name the event that most confirmed your faith in the human spirit, what would it be?

⊷⊶ ⊫⬦⊨ ⊷⊶

If you had to name something that always seems to call or speak to your soul, what would you say?

⊷⊶ ⊫⬦⊨ ⊷⊶

If you wanted to meditate for a whole day, where would you do it?

If you had to pick the most important value you hold, what would it be?

If you found yourself on a crashing airplane, what thought do you expect would first come to mind?

⇥◆⇤

If you had to give one example of how your nation shows its moral fiber, what would it be?

⇥◆⇤

If you were to identify one aspect of your behavior that masks your insecurities, what would it be?

⇥◆⇤

If you were to finish the sentence "My destiny has always been . . . ," how would it end?

If you were to name the zodiac signs that you are most and least compatible with, what would they be?

⚊⚊ ⚌✦⚌ ⚊⚊

If you were to take a look at the various "guilts" that you carry around with you, which would be least justified, and which would be most justified?

⚊⚊ ⚌✦⚌ ⚊⚊

If you were asked where and how you learned to love, what would you say?

⚊⚊ ⚌✦⚌ ⚊⚊

If you had to name the event that most challenged your faith in the human soul, what would you say?

If you could witness a miracle, what would you choose to see?

—— ≡✦≡ ——

If you had to name the most spiritual building you have entered, which would you choose?

If you were to name one person you have known in your life that you honestly felt morally inferior to, who would you name?

—— ≡✦≡ ——

If you were to name one person you have known in your life that you honestly felt morally superior to, who would it be?

If you were to complete the sentence "We were put on this earth to . . . ," how would you finish it?

If you had to pick one man-made item to be the symbol for a new religion, what would it be?

If you were to name the single most painful experience in life, what would it be?

If you were to name the single most challenging aspect of life, what would you say?

If you had to name an ethical role model in your life, who would it be?

If you had to name the person you found it most difficult to forgive for something, who was it, and what for?

If you were to name one thing for which you could never forgive someone, even a loved one, what would it be?

If you were to cite an example that defined "trust" for you, what would it be?

If you were to cite an example that defined "goodness" for you, what would you say?

If you had to pick the least appropriate thing to pray for, what would you say it is?

If you were to name a person you have known who exemplified weakness of character, who would it be?

If you were to name someone you know who best personifies strength of character, who would it be?

If you could be the psychologist for anyone you know, who would you select?

If you were to name the two sides of your personality that are most contradictory, what would you say?

＋・＝＋＝・＋

If you could determine the last thing you see before your own death, what would it be?

＋・＝＋＝・＋

If you could have one thing said about you by everyone after your death, what would you want them to say?

41

If you were to name a person who surprised you most with their strength of character, who would it be?

If you had to select one thing you wish you hadn't witnessed or experienced in your life, what would you say it was?

If you had to name the most difficult thing for you to talk about, what would it be? (You don't have to talk about it, just name it.)

If you could have one experience before dying that you've never had, what would it be?

If you were to name the person you've had a continuous psychological power struggle with, who would it be?

·—·   ≡◊≡   ·—·

If you were to name a time when your body and mind were at odds with each other, when would it be?

·—·   ≡◊≡   ·—·

If you had to name your biggest contribution to helping mankind, what would you say?

·—·   ≡◊≡   ·—·

If you were to describe your fantasy of a transcendental experience, what would it be like?

If you were to name the music that has touched your soul the most deeply, what would it be?

If God were to appear briefly before you in any form you chose, what would it be?

If you had to define the circumstances under which it is ethically right to lie, what would they be?

If you had to describe the circumstances under which it would be ethically proper to break the law, what would you say?

If you had to have one religious leader to dinner tonight, who would you invite?

If you were to define the criteria necessary to justify the taking of human life, what would they be?

If you were to determine what life's greatest adventure is, what would you say?

If you were to become a telephone counselor in a crisis center, what type of personal crisis do you think would be the most difficult to deal with?

If you could say one thing to a religious leader in the world, who would you pick, and what would you say?

—+—≡◇≡—+—

If you were in personal crisis yourself, who among your friends would you first turn to for moral support?

—+—≡◇≡—+—

If you were to describe your life right now as a hallway with six closed doors, what signs would you put on the three doors that you want to open, and on the three doors that you want to keep locked?

—+—≡◇≡—+—

If you could remove three barriers in your life that prevent you from realizing your dreams, what would they be?

If you were to be asked one question that would be the most revealing or difficult to answer, what would it be?

—⟨⟩—

If you were to cite an experience that truly makes you feel insignificant in the larger sense of the universe, what would you say it is?

If you were to name a period in your life when you most relied on religion or faith for strength, when would you say it was?

—⟨⟩—

If there was a time in your life that required you to search most deeply for your own inner strength, when would it be?

If you found out today that you are immortal, how would you change your life?

⊶ ⊷

If you found out that a close friend of yours had done something in the past that you found morally reprehensible, what would you do?

⊶ ⊷

If you were to say that there are things in life you truly deserve, what would you name?

⊶ ⊷

If you could change one thing in your own life to make it more balanced, what would it be?

48

If you were to be visited by the ghost of someone who lived in the past, who would you prefer it to be?

If aliens were to visit your house and offered to take you with them on their spaceship but could not guarantee your return, what would you do?

If you were offered immortality on Earth in exchange for one substantial thing, what would you be willing to offer?

If you could learn one thing (but only one thing) about your own death right now, what would you want it to be?

If you could have prevented one religious event, which one would you pick?

—+ ≡◊≡ +—

If you were to define what true personal freedom is, what would you say?

—+ ≡◊≡ +—

If you were to tragically die tomorrow, who, other than blood relatives, would you want to raise your children?

—+ ≡◊≡ +—

If you made a very big mistake of some kind, who, of the people you know, would you first confess it to?

50

If you had to name the thing you are most curious about in another religion, what would it be?

————— ⋈◊⋈ —————

If you could determine one new law to be passed that would address a moral issue, what would it be?

————— ⋈◊⋈ —————

If you found out you were terminally ill and could do one thing to put your soul in order, what would it be?

If you could have the chance, when you die, to repent for only one thing, what would you choose?

If you had to give a one-word answer to the question "Why is life worth living," what would it be?

If you could erase one thing from your conscience, what would it be?

If you had to select the most important human emotion, which would you single out?

If you were to name the person you have known who brought out the deepest feelings in you (other than love), who would it be?

If you were responsible for casting a new film about Jesus Christ, which current actor would you give the role to?

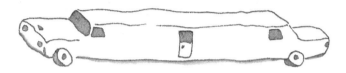

If you decided to rid yourself of all your possessions but one for the sake of cleansing your soul, what single thing would you keep?

＋—＝◆＝—＋

If you found yourself in a period of deep depression, which of your current possessions would best help you endure it?

＋—＝◆＝—＋

If you were to recall a time or situation in your life when prayer was the most helpful, when would you say it was?

If you were to describe a way in which the soul of a person is tested, what would it be?

If you were to describe your attitude toward sin, what would you say?

If you could ask a psychic one question, knowing you would get a true answer, what would you ask?

If a psychic offered to tell you anything you wanted to know about your life, what is the thing you would *least* like to know about?

54

If you were to name the couple that most fully complete and complement each other, who would they be?

If you were to determine the primary issue that the majority of people confront in each decade of their life (e.g., their twenties, their thirties, etc. . . .), what would you answer?

If you were to choose the person who has a true aura of calm around them, who would it be?

If you were to name the person you know with the healthiest philosophy about life, who would it be?

If you wanted to prove your trustworthiness to someone you know, how would you do it?

If you had to recall a time in your life when your self-esteem was at its highest, when would you say it was?

If one thing were to happen right now that would be the most damaging to your confidence, what would it be?

If one thing could happen right now that would most effectively boost your confidence, what would it be?

If you had to elect the time when your ego took the biggest blow, when would it be?

If you had to name the person you know who is most afraid of their own mortality, who would it be?

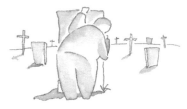

If you had to name the person you know who is most at ease with their own mortality, who would it be?

If you had to cite the moment in your life when you came closest to encountering true evil, when would you say it was?

If you unexpectedly found yourself in Hell after dying, who, among the people you have known, would you be the least surprised to find there as well?

———— ≡♦≡ ————

If you had to choose one of your current friends or acquaintances to be the only person who would know your entire personal history of sin, who would you pick?

———— ≡♦≡ ————

If you were to name the most profound religious ritual you know of, what would it be?

———— ≡♦≡ ————

If you were to name an omen or sign that helped you choose a path in your life, what would you say?

If you were to choose the person who is most like you emotionally, who would it be?

If you were to name the most creative outlet that you have, what would it be?

If you were to point to a place on your body that you would say is the center of your emotional being, what spot would you pick?

If you could say one thing to God, what would you say?

If you had to learn about every sin one person you know has committed or will ever commit, who would you choose?

If you were to name what you think mankind's most positive characteristic is, what would you say?

If you were to name what you think mankind's most negative enduring characteristic is, what would it be?

If you were to be reincarnated and could choose your next physical form, who or what would you come back as?

If you were to spend eternity as a ghost on Earth, who or what would you haunt?

＋・＝◆＝・＋

If you could have your ashes scattered on any body of water on Earth, which would you choose?

If you were to name the teacher who had the greatest positive influence on your character, who would it be?

＋・＝◆＝・＋

If you were to surmise the secret of a tranquil soul, what would it be?

If you had to describe the issue about which you most disagree with in any single religion, what would it be?

⚜

If you had to name the issue about which you most disagree with in your own religion, what would it be?

⚜

If you were to name the most difficult thing morally that you could ever be asked to do, what would it be?

⚜

If you were to choose the single most joyous thing about life, what would it be?

If you could change one thing about your family situation to bring it peace and more happiness, what would it be?

If you were to name the one thing in life that you are most faithful to, other than religion, what would it be?

—————

If you had to remember the moment in your life when you felt most alone, when would it be?

—————

If you were to recall the most providential moment or experience in your life, what would you say?

If you were to cite the moment or age in your life when you were truly happiest, when would it be?

If you had to relate the most humiliating experience of your life, what would it be?

If you were to describe the moment of your life when you felt the proudest of yourself, what would you say?

If you were to recall the moment of your life when you felt the proudest of someone else, when would it be?

If you were to complete the phrase "I love my life when . . . ," how would you finish it?

————— ⊯ ——

If you were to name one person whose tranquillity you most envy or admire, who would it be?

————— ⊯ ——

If you were to leave one thing you have to your religion when you die (other than money), what would you give?

If you were to pick the moment of each day that you feel most serene, when would it be?

If you were to pick the moment of the day when you feel most agitated, when would it be?

If you could remove one hindrance to your own spiritual well-being, what would it be?

If there was one dream for your life that you didn't follow, what would you say it was?

If you were to name the person who is furthest from their calling and destiny in life, who would you choose?

If you found out that you were terminally ill and could make one journey anywhere in the world to help ease your soul, where would you go?

If you had to name the source of highest authority in your life, who or what would it be?

＋—─ ⅀◆⅀ —＋

If you were to name the most powerful vision you have ever had, what would it be?

＋—─ ⅀◆⅀ —＋

If you decided to become an evangelist, which state would you base yourself in?

If you had to state the most important belief you hold, what would it be?

If there was one primary law or principle you lived by, what would you say it was?

If you were about to be executed and could make one statement to be broadcast to the entire world, what would you say?

If you were to finish the phrase "I have been blessed because . . . ," how would it end?

If you had to cite the worst example of disloyalty or betrayed trust that you know of, what would it be?

If you were to recall the biggest error you have ever made in the judgment of character, when would you say it was?

If you were to name the person you have known personally who comes the closest to being a religious fanatic, who would it be?

If you could have one of the current U.S. Supreme Court justices removed because of their moral positions, which one would it be?

69

If you had to name the thing that has been the most difficult for you to give up, what would it be?

If you were to articulate the most important thing missing from your life right now, what would you say?

If you were to cite one supreme example of loyalty, what would it be?

If you had to name the one thing you care about most in life (other than another human being), what would it be?

If you could relieve yourself of one burden in life, what would it be?

If you could relieve your spouse of one burden in life, what would you take away?

If you were to name the best example you know of evil masquerading as good, what would it be?

If you were to make a collage of symbols as a visual way of describing yourself to someone, what would it include?

If you were to say when it is that you normally have the most self-confidence, when would it be?

If you died and could look back on your life, what is the one thing you think you'd miss the most?

If you had to name the best thing about getting older, what would you say it is?

If you were to have been a mystic hermit, where and when in history would you like to have lived?

72

If you were to change your life in one way to make it "more Zen," how would you do it?

If you were to name the event that changed your relationship with your family the most, what would you choose?

If you were to admit the thing you consistently delude yourself about, what would it be?

If you were to spend 15 minutes a day just "thinking" as a way to make you emotionally stronger, what would you concentrate your thoughts on?

If you had been a disciple of one religious prophet in history, who would you want to have followed?

—+— ☒✦☒ —+—

If you had to choose the year of your life when you were the most truly content, how old would you have been at the time?

—+— ☒✦☒ —+—

If you could have more ambition in a single area of your life, what would it be?

—+— ☒✦☒ —+—

If you had to name a friend whose ambition hurts them more than it helps, who would you say it is?

74

If you were to select a person whose persona does not fit their body type, who would it be?

If you believe that it was destiny to be born to your parents, what would you use as an example to prove it?

If you were to name a time when your body and mind worked best together to make something happen, when would it be?

If you could eliminate one source of anger in your life right now, what would it be?

75

If you had to remember one occasion when you were unjustly angry, when would it be?

—+— ≒÷≒ —+—

If you could eliminate the anger in someone you know and replace it with inner peace, who would you choose?

—+— ≒÷≒ —+—

If you had to define the relation between beauty and goodness (if any), what would you say?

—+— ≒÷≒ —+—

If you had to somehow place your moral life in the care of someone else, who would it be?

If you had to cite an example from your experience when beauty masked evil, when would you say it was?

If you were to name a person you have known whose inner goodness truly rendered them beautiful, even if conventionally they were not considered so, who would it be?

If you had to say what you associate the sound of ringing bells with, what would it be?

If there was one time in your life you wish, in retrospect, that you had been more open with someone, when would you say it was?

77

If you had to confess the worst sin you have ever committed, what would you say?

If there was an occasion in your life when you wish you had used less candor, when would it be?

If you had to name a time when you wish someone in particular had used more candor with you, when would you say it was?

If you were to name the most caring person you have ever known, who would it be?

If you could awaken one aspect of your personality that you had as a child and feel that you have since lost, what would it be?

—+— ⬕◈⬔ —+—

If you could follow your heart right now and do one thing that you otherwise wouldn't be inclined to do, what would it be?

—+— ⬕◈⬔ —+—

If you could transmit some of your positive energy to any place on the planet, where would you send it?

If you were to become a TV evangelist, what would you call yourself?

If you read in tomorrow's newspaper that someone you know personally had given their life for a cause, who would it most likely be, and for what?

﹡﹗﹡﹗﹡

If you had to name the one thing in life that is generally the cause of unhappiness, what would you say it is?

﹡﹗﹡﹗﹡

If you had to name the one thing in life that is generally the source of happiness, what would it be?

﹡﹗﹡﹗﹡

If you were to name three people throughout your life that helped to complete you as a person, who would they be?

If you were to describe the physical qualities of Paradise the way you want it to be, what would it look like?

If you could witness one supernatural event, what would you want it to be?

＋━＋ ▨◈▨ ＋━＋

If you were to name the person who leads the most beautiful life, who would it be?

＋━＋ ▨◈▨ ＋━＋

If you were to act out all of the seven deadly sins, what specific things would you do for each of them?

If you were to name the person you know who is building up the worst karma, who would it be?

If you could possess one quality that you don't presently have, what would it be?

If you had to name your worst character trait, what would you say it is?

If you had to choose one character trait of your own that you most hope your children will possess, what would it be?

If you had to name the most difficult spiritual concept to understand, what would it be?

———— ⌖⌖⌖ ————

If you had to identify the fairest religion, which would you say it is?

———— ⌖⌖⌖ ————

If you were to pray in front of anything once a day, what would it be?

If you were to name a place where you have felt the most rooted, where would it be?

If you were to name one person who you have felt closest to in spirit, who would it be?

If you were to choose one holy day that represents the best qualities of your own religion, which would it be?

If you were to define the term "soul mate," how would you do it?

If you named the person you know who lives the most Zen-like existence, who would it be?

84

If you were to name your biggest fear, what would you say it is?

If you were to select the person most in touch with their own feelings, who would it be?

＋＋　▤◆▤　＋＋

If you were to say there is a person who truly practices what they preach, who would it be?

＋＋　▤◆▤　＋＋

If you were to console one person who needs comforting right now, who would it be?

If you were to name the most important thing in your life right now, what would it be?

If you were to give yourself one piece of advice about your own beliefs or lack thereof, what would it be?

If you could have more faith in one thing, what would it be?

If you were to name the most comforting place to be touched by another's hands, where would it be?

If you had to name the emotion that resides deepest inside of you, what would it be?

If you were to define the difference between fate and destiny, what would you say?

If the eyes are the windows to your soul, whose reveal the most?

If there was one road in life you should not have gone down but did, which would it be?

If you were to compare your own soul to that of an animal, what species would match the best?

If you were to bare your soul to one person you know, who would you choose?

If you had to cite the one thing that tested your moral judgment the most, what would you say it was?

If you were to name the emotion that you waste the most time on, what would it be?

If you were to recall one situation in your experience where you would rather not have known the truth, when would it be?

If you were to name the most mysterious phenomenon you have ever witnessed, what would it be?

If you could name seven wonders of the spiritual realm, what would they be?

If you could visit one religious site in the world, where would you go?

If you found out for certain that fate accounts for every aspect of your life, how would your attitude toward life change?

———— ✠ ————

If you could have any person or people around you at the moment of your death, who would you have?

———— ✠ ————

If you were to make a religious site out of a place that currently isn't one, which would it be, and for what religion?

———— ✠ ————

If you were to define what truly constitutes a lost soul, what would you say?

If you had to name the religion that is the most concerned with the present (as opposed to the afterlife), which would it be?

If you could put a curse on anyone you know, who would get it?

If you were to name the thing you have the most compassion for, what would it be?

If you were to pick one conundrum to contemplate for your whole life, what would it be?

If you had to choose the species of animal that you think would make the best symbol of evil, which would you select?

——— ⊰⊱ ———

If you were to elect one animal species to be the symbol of goodness, which would it be?

——— ⊰⊱ ———

If there were one road in life that you should have taken but didn't, what would it be?

——— ⊰⊱ ———

If you set out to purify your own soul, how would you go about it?

If you could let go of one of your most destructive ambitions, what would it be?

━━ ⊫✦⊨ ━━

If you were to describe what makes a person truly virtuous, what would you say?

━━ ⊫✦⊨ ━━

If you were to describe the path you have followed in life, what would you say?

If you were to have one entertainer at your funeral, who would you choose?

If you were to name the most peaceful place in nature that you have ever seen, where would it be?

⋯ ⋙✦⋙ ⋯

If you were to start your own religion, what would you call it, and what would be its mission?

⋯ ⋙✦⋙ ⋯

If you had to explain to a person from another planet what religion is, how would you do it?

⋯ ⋙✦⋙ ⋯

If you were to name your least developed emotion, what would it be?

If you were to make an argument for the presence of destiny in everyone's life, what examples would you use?

＋＋ ≡♦≡ ＋＋

If you had to make an argument *against* the idea of destiny, what would you say?

＋＋ ≡♦≡ ＋＋

If you had to predict the next big choice that life will present to you, what would it be?

If there is one person you know whose eyes tell the most about their inner self, what do they reveal?

If you were to pick the person whose demeanor and expression reveal the least about their inner feelings, who would it be?

--- ✠ ---

If you were suddenly compelled to go on a spiritual journey, where do you think it would take you, and what would it entail?

--- ✠ ---

If there was one aspect of your life that you could possibly be persecuted for, what would it be?

--- ✠ ---

If you were asked what your "mind, body, and soul" mean in your own life, what would you say?

96

If there was a dream you've had that illuminated something from your past, which would it be?

~ ~ ~

If you had to name a person who is the most intuitive of the people you know, who would it be?

If you were to qualify your own spiritual aspirations, what would you say they are?

~ ~ ~

If you were to choose a time in history when mankind made true spiritual progress, when would it be?

If you were to rejoice for one particular thing in your life right now, what would it be?

—+— ≡✦≡ —+—

If you were asked how your religion has shaped your personality, what would you say?

—+— ≡✦≡ —+—

If there was one thing that you do consistently in order to be accepted by others, what would you say it was?

—+— ≡✦≡ —+—

If there is one burden in life that should be shared by all, what would you say it is?

If you were to name a situation in which your heart and mind were truly in synch, what would you say?

If you were to name a person you know who would most benefit from meditation, who would it be?

If you had to admit to the most selfish thing you do on a regular basis, what would you say?

If you could proclaim the least selfish thing you do on a regular basis, what would it be?

If you were to name the person you know who is the most able to look at themselves objectively, who would it be?

⊷ ⋈⊹⋊ ⊶

If you were to name the person who is the best at getting down to the heart of things when talking about life issues, who would it be?

⊷ ⋈⊹⋊ ⊶

If you had to pick the civilization or society that has lived the most harmoniously with nature, which would it be?

⊷ ⋈⊹⋊ ⊶

If God appeared and said to you, "Tell me something I don't know," what would you say?

100

If you were to describe how myths play a role in modern life, what would you say?

⊷⊶ ▨◊▨ ⊷⊶

If you were to select the religious symbol that means the most to you personally, what would you choose?

⊷⊶ ▨◊▨ ⊷⊶

If you could be the Devil for a day, what would you do?

If you had to pick an occasion when your subconscious gave you the best guidance, when would it be?

If you were to come up with a marking on the human body for a new religion, what would you propose?

If you had to name the person you know who inspires your strongest sympathies, who would it be?

If you were to design a room for contemplation, what would it look like, and what would be in it?

If you were to name the most spiritual piece of art that you have seen, what would it be?

102

If there were to be a new promised land, where would you predict it to be located?

If you were to name one person you know who has truly found their destiny, who would it be?

If you were to name a time when you looked in the mirror and saw yourself as a stranger, when would it be?

If you discovered that you had exactly one year/month/week to live, what would you do, and who is the first person you'd tell?

If there is one burden that no person should have to bear alone, what would you say it is?

If you were to pick one dream you've had that came the closest to coming true, which was it?

If you were to meditate with one other person, who would you choose?

If you were to name a situation when your heart and mind were truly at odds, when would it be?

104

If you were to recall the time when a good cry had the most therapeutic effect on you, when would it be?

If you could edit out one recurring thought that occupies your mind, what would it be?

＋－　≡✦≡　－＋

If you were to name the healthiest thoughts you have on a daily basis, what would they be?

＋－　≡✦≡　－＋

If you were to propose that every person in the world do one thing every day for 15 minutes to better the world, what would you have them do?

If you had to name a person who is your alter ego, who would it be?

⚜

If you were to recommend only one book to a friend to help them find spirituality, which would it be?

⚜

If you were to remember one time when you truly transcended your material life, when would you say it was?

⚜

If you had to choose one person who truly gets energy from their religion or faith, who would it be?

106

If you were to describe the most notable way that the moon affects you, what would you say?

If you were to select the one characteristic of your zodiac sign that most fits your personality, what would it be?

———— ≍♦≍ ————

If you could reconcile with the person who is your biggest enemy, how would you do it?

———— ≍♦≍ ————

If you were to name a religious conflict in which there is truly no fair solution, what would it be?

If you were to complete the sentence "I hate myself when . . . ," how would it end?

If you could go back and ask Buddha one question, what would it be?

If you could ask Allah one thing, what would it be?

If you were to name the best method for teaching your children moral values, what would you say it is?

If you were to finish the statement "A perfect human being is . . . ," how would it end?

If you were to determine the single most important family value, what would you say it is?

If you were to pick a spiritual place to get married (other than a religious structure), where would it be?

If you could serve as a functionary of any religious order, what would you be, and which religion would you serve?

If you were to go on a mission for any religious cause, where would you want to go, and what would your mission be?

If you were to choose the three things that you most value about your own religion, what would you say?

If you were to list three things that you would most like to reform in your own religion, what would they be?

If you were to name an aspect of your own personality that you have the most difficulty explaining to other people, what would it be?

If you were to select the person who is the most hypocritical about their own religion, who would you choose?

If you were to choose a person who you think should convert to another religion, who would it be?

If you could bring back one deceased relative to see one thing, who would you choose, and what would you show them?

If you could have eased the death of one person, whose would you have chosen?

If you could teach your own children the most important aspects of their religious heritage, what would you say they are?

If you were to tailor Heaven to your needs, what would it be like?

If you were to name the emotion that has grown strongest as you have gotten older, what would it be?

If you were to identify an emotion that has decreased in importance for you over time, what would it be?

If you were to remember the most powerful moment of silence you have ever experienced, when would it be?

— ⊠ —

If you were to recall the time in life when you felt most vulnerable, when would it be?

— ⊠ —

If you could take more control of one aspect of your own life, what would it be?

If you were to state the difference between the male soul and the female soul, what would you say?

If you could have one person understand you better, who would you pick?

—— ⽷✦⽷ ——

If you were to select your favorite story from the Bible, what would it be?

—— ⽷✦⽷ ——

If you could dream about one aspect of your life more, what would you want it to be?

—— ⽷✦⽷ ——

If you could have one person experience a dream that you have had, who would you pick, and what dream would it be?

If you could have an angel whisper one thing in your ear every day, what would you want to hear?

If you were to plant any type of tree over your body or ashes when you die, what type would you choose?

If you heard someone described as a "good soul," what would you assume that meant?

If you were to choose your own pallbearers, who would they be?

If you were to recall the most painful experience you have had involving a sibling, what would it be?

If you were to remember the best experience you have had regarding a sibling, what would it be?

If you were to name someone whose death has affected you most, who would it be?

If you had to control the destiny of any one person, who would it be?

If you were to name the worst consequences of organized religion, what would they be?

If you were to say that there is one aspect common to all religions, what would it be?

If you were to be the Devil, what would your outfit look like?

If you had seven days to create the world, what would *you* do on each of those seven days?

If you had to give control of your destiny to any person, who would get it?

If you could focus more energy on one part of your life, what would it be?

If you were to decide the most important thing to do on your birthday, what would it be?

If you were to state the secret for aging contentedly, what would you say?

If you had to name the topic that is the most painful to discuss with your parents, what would it be?

If you were to name the one personality flaw you have that you will never be able to overcome, what would you say it is?

If you had to design your own true Hell, what would it be like?

If you could alter other people's perception of you, what would you change?

119

If you were to give significance to each of the four elements (earth, water, fire, and air) in your own life, what would you say?

If you were to name a period in your life when you thought about death the most, when would it be?

If you were to say there has been a person in your life who has been your symbolic lighthouse, who would it be?

If you were to design your own mausoleum, what would it look like?

If you were to cite the worst stereotype associated with your religion, what would you say?

—+— ⊱✦⊰ —+—

If you were to say that there is a period of your past life that you dream or think the most about, when would it be?

—+— ⊱✦⊰ —+—

If you were to choose a time when your imagination was at its best, when would it be?

—+— ⊱✦⊰ —+—

If you were to name one person who interprets dreams particularly well, who would it be?

121

If you were to become a TV evangelist, how would you do your hair?

If you were to name a religion that is truly loony, which would it be?

If after you die your spirit could protect anyone in the world, who would you pick?

If you could find out the truth about any one thing, what would you ask about?

If you could have a sudden surge of inspiration for one thing in your life, what would you want it to be for?

If you were to recall a dream that helped you solve a problem or see things more clearly, what would it be?

If you were to identify an event where the power of the crowd was truly inspiring, what would it be?

If you were to name the most comforting thing for you to hold in your hands, what would it be?

123

If you were to sail around the world for a spiritual experience with one person other than your spouse or lover, who would you pick as your companion?

If you could teach one person a lesson in humility, who would it be?

＊＊＊

If you were to fast for any cause, which would you choose?

＊＊＊

If you were to name a person you know who could most likely be a monk, who would it be?

If you were to say that there was one person you know who has supernatural powers, who would it most likely be?

If you could have the characters in any painting come to life, which painting would you choose?

If you were to describe an out-of-body experience that you have had, what would you say?

If you could have more patience in one aspect of your life, what would it be?

If you had to identify the most normal thing about yourself, what would it be?

If you confessed the most abnormal thing about yourself, what would you say?

If you were to say that there is one area of your life in which you always follow your heart over your head, what would it be?

If you were to be displayed after death in an open coffin for a number of days, and you could have one thing in there with you, what would you want it to be?

If you were to leave instructions for what music would be played at your funeral or wake, what would they be?

—— ≡♦≡ ——

If you could know the whereabouts of anyone's soul, whose would you ask about?

—— ≡♦≡ ——

If you could add one annual religious holiday, what would it be for, and when would it be?

—— ≡♦≡ ——

If you were to name the biggest contribution that organized religion makes to better the world, what would it be?

If you were to write a living will right now, what would it say?

⸻ ≡◆≡ ⸻

If you had to experience one trauma that your mother had to go through in order to understand her better, what would you pick?

⸻ ≡◆≡ ⸻

If you had to articulate the biggest misunderstanding between you and your parents, what would you say?

If you were to pick something from nature to be the symbol of a new religion, what would it be?

If you had to define the single biggest threat or impediment to the spiritual life, what would you say?

If you were to select the person you know with the most imbalanced life, who would it be?

If you had to name the most moral political leader in power today, who would it be?

If you were God for one day, what would you do?

If you have an interesting or humorous question or answer to contribute to sequels in the *If . . .* series, we would love to hear from you. Please send your response or new question to the address below. Please give us your name and age, and sign and date your contribution. Thank you.

Evelyn McFarlane
James Saywell
c/o Villard Books
201 East 50th Street
New York, NY 10022

E-mail: author@ifbooks.com
Website: http://www.ifbooks.com

About the Authors

EVELYN MCFARLANE was born in Brooklyn and grew up in San Diego. She received a degree in architecture from Cornell University and has worked in New York and Boston as an architect. She now lives in Florence, Italy. In addition to writing, she lectures on architecture for the Elder Hostel programs and is a full-time student at the Florence Academy of Art.

JAMES SAYWELL was born in Canada and lived in Asia as a child. Besides questions, he designs buildings and furniture. He divides his time between the United States and Italy.